AF604981

99 THINGS THAT REALLY ANNOY US OLD GUYS

99 THINGS THAT REALLY ANNOY US OLD GUYS

CARTOONS BY
MARTIN WAKEMAN

First published in 2024 by New Holland Publishers
Sydney

Level 1, 178 Fox Valley Road, Wahroonga, NSW 2076, Australia

newhollandpublishers.com

A record of this book is held at the National Library of Australia.

ISBN 9781760796723

Managing Director: Fiona Schultz
Designer: Andrew Davies
Production Director: Arlene Gippert
Printed in China

Keep up with New Holland Publishers:
NewHollandPublishers
@newhollandpublishers

I've become a grumpy old git.

As I grow older more and more things are beginning to irritate me.

And some things really really piss me off.

I'm sure I'm not the only old guy to experience this.

So, as a form of therapy I've decided to create this series of 99 cartoons of just some of the things that really annoy me.

And I hope that some of these cartoons will also strike a chord with many of my fellow oldies. If they don't then perhaps its only me that needs therapy.

Have fun and enjoy the book.

Martin Wakeman

THINGS THAT REALLY ANNOY US OLD GUYS No. 1

People who throw litter in my garden.

When I put something down just a minute ago and now I can't find it.

Traffic jams.

THINGS THAT REALLY ANNOY US OLD GUYS No. **4**

People who insist on squeezing into the first available parking space.

THINGS THAT REALLY ANNOY US OLD GUYS No. **5**

Neighbours.

A faulty toilet lid
dropping down mid-pee.

When strangers talk to me
at inappropriate moments.

Forgetting my reading glasses.

THINGS THAT REALLY ANNOY US OLD GUYS No. **9**

When somebody stops suddenly
in front of me on a crowded street.

THINGS THAT REALLY ANNOY US OLD GUYS No. **10**

When the instructions are in small print and difficult to find amongst the safety warnings.

Stores that reorganise shelves
so that I can't find anything.

Losing the remote just as the programme is about to start.

THINGS THAT REALLY ANNOY US OLD GUYS No. **13**

Stubbing my toe.

THINGS THAT REALLY ANNOY US OLD GUYS No. **14**

Tight shoes.

THINGS THAT REALLY ANNOY US OLD GUYS No. **15**

Hair growing in places it shouldn't.

When my clothes shrink in the wardrobe since the last time I wore them.

THINGS THAT REALLY ANNOY US OLD GUYS No. **17**

When the tool I want
is just out of reach.

Someone sniffing loudly
instead of blowing their nose.

People who put bags on seats then pretend they didn't notice you.

When I politely open the coffee shop door for someone and they proceed to order for the entire office.

THINGS THAT REALLY ANNOY US OLD GUYS No. **21**

People using their phones on loud speaker so you can hear both sides of the conversation.

THINGS THAT REALLY ANNOY US OLD GUYS No. **22**

When a shit just won't happen.

Reaching the top of the stairs then not remembering what I came up here for.

Meeting up with someone and not being able to remember their name.

THINGS THAT REALLY ANNOY US OLD GUYS No. **25**

Sticky price labels that
just won't peel off.

THINGS THAT REALLY ANNOY US OLD GUYS No. **26**

Losing the end of the sellotape roll.

Having to remove shoes, belt, jacket etc. When I obviously don't look like a terrorist.

Screaming babies.

THINGS THAT REALLY ANNOY US OLD GUYS No. **29**

People who read over your shoulder.

Waiters who ignore me.

Inconsiderate parking.

Truck drivers who drive two inches from your back windscreen.

THINGS THAT REALLY ANNOY US OLD GUYS No. **33**

Milk cartons.

Shops that don't provide seats outside changing rooms.

Electric shavers that run out of power.

Vending machines that don't deliver.

ITS A CHATEAU LA MER 2001. A PARTICULARLY GOOD YEAR IN A WINE NOTED FOR ITS PETULANT NAÏVETÉ
PLONK

Wine snobs.

Golf!

Telephone salespeople.

Push-down taps that pop up immediately you let go.

People who don't let you out of a lift before they get in.

People who don't turn the tv off
when I visit.

Supermarket trolleys.

THINGS THAT REALLY ANNOY US OLD GUYS No. **44**

Queues that move faster than mine.

THINGS THAT REALLY ANNOY US OLD GUYS No. **45**

People taking ages to check in.

Stores that start
Christmas in September.

Showers that won't stay
at one temperature.

Childproof caps.

THINGS THAT REALLY ANNOY US OLD GUYS No. **49**

People who park outside my house.

THINGS THAT REALLY ANNOY US OLD GUYS No. **50**

Flat-pack furniture.

THINGS THAT REALLY ANNOY US OLD GUYS No. **51**

Barbecues that won't light.

Contemporaries of mine
who are not losing their hair.

People who can't control their bladders.

Neighbours who want to chat
when you're trying to rush.

THINGS THAT REALLY ANNOY US OLD GUYS No. **55**

Sinks that splash back leaving
an embarrassing wet patch.

Loud people in restaurants.

Toilet paper dispensers that only give out one sheet at a time.

People who take ages to
choose what they want.

THINGS THAT REALLY ANNOY US OLD GUYS No. **59**

Little old ladies who
invade my personal space.

Crowds of people shopping
when I want to shop.

Waiting in for a late delivery.

When you are in a hurry and your computer starts updating.

When you risk a fart and realise
you have suffered a follow through.

THINGS THAT REALLY ANNOY US OLD GUYS No. **64**

Football referees.

When you snuggle down to sleep
but realise you want to pee.

People who impose their
musical tastes on everyone else.

THINGS THAT REALLY ANNOY US OLD GUYS No. **67**

An unflushed toilet.

Biting the inside of
your cheek whilst eating.

Phone scammers and phone companies that don't do anything to stop them.

Small stones in my shoe.

THINGS THAT REALLY ANNOY US OLD GUYS No. 71

Yappy dogs.

Having to make small talk with strangers who I'll never meet again in my lifetime.

Aches and pains that last for ages.

How difficult it is to lose weight.

THINGS THAT REALLY ANNOY US OLD GUYS No. **75**

How easy it is to gain weight.

When you wake up in the night
and you can't get back to sleep.

THINGS THAT REALLY ANNOY US OLD GUYS No. **77**

Cramp in the night.

When you realise you are adding sound effects when you are putting on your socks.

THINGS THAT REALLY ANNOY US OLD GUYS No. **79**

When your zip gets stuck.

Smokers who stub out cigarette butts expecting someone else will clean them up.

THINGS THAT REALLY ANNOY US OLD GUYS No. **81**

People who throw litter out of cars.

THINGS THAT REALLY ANNOY US OLD GUYS No. **82**

Having to stock loads of different light bulbs because they all have different fittings.

THINGS THAT REALLY ANNOY US OLD GUYS No. **83**

Over-enthusiastic sales people.

The same old Christmas songs being played endlessly year after year.

Parents who don't control
their children.

When every light in the house
is left on.

Self-service checkouts.

Cyclists.

Restaurants that are too dark.

Spilling stuff down
my going-out shirt.

Airports that have hard
and uncomfortable seats.

THINGS THAT REALLY ANNOY US OLD GUYS No. **92**

People who take ages
in the airplane toilets.

THINGS THAT REALLY ANNOY US OLD GUYS No. **93**

Moist toilet seats.

Breakfast show hosts that
are just tooooo bright.

Dogs who sniff your crotch.

An unflushable turd.

THINGS THAT REALLY ANNOY US OLD GUYS No. **97**

People who visit in the middle of my favourite programme.

THINGS THAT REALLY ANNOY US OLD GUYS No. **98**

Hand driers that are as powerful as a gnat's fart.

THINGS THAT REALLY ANNOY US OLD GUYS No. **99**

Guests who won't leave when I'm tired.